LAST TRAVELS
BEFORE
THE LOCKDOWNS

Russell Evans

CONTENTS

INTRODUCTION 1

PART 1   *Rhine River Cruise in June 2017* *3*

PART 2   *United Arab Emirates (UAE) in November 2017* *37*

PART 3   *Canada in August – September 2018* *84*

INTRODUCTION

I started to write this Introduction looking out onto a wet and windy and quite a cold winter's day in England in February 2023.

The winter here has not yet become spring, and so it is good to remember the previous sunny holidays and times, such as are described on the following pages! There are many photographs to be seen and not too many words to be read.

The years of 2017 and 2018 were the last recent years when we (and the rest of the world during the lockdowns) were fully up to such relatively carefree overseas holidays, but hopefully better times will return. My mobility was badly impaired in the early summer of 2019 with knee problems. Heather and I downsized to a new smaller home in late 2019, and then of course the worldwide Covid-19 pandemic hit us all at the end of 2019 and continued during 2020 and for several years later.

Subsequent pages are organised into three parts. Part 1 covers our one-week river cruise in June 2017, along the Rhine and Moselle Rivers in Germany. This packaged holiday was arranged with Riviera Travel – the UK based Tours and Cruises company. One highlight of this trip was to meet up for most of a day in the riverside village of Rudesheim (on the banks of the southern river Rhine) with Heather's cousin Pat Hoos, who lives in Germany with members of her family nearby and who manages to visit the UK now and then.

Part 2 covers our one-week visit to the UAE (United Arab Emirates) in the Middle East in November 2017. This packaged holiday was arranged with the UK office of RSD Travel, the multi-national (and low cost!) European travel company. There were some difficulties along the way with the night flights via Istanbul in Turkey and with several different hotels being stayed at, but we felt we made a proper recognition of our 40th Wedding Anniversary by returning to the Middle East, where we had spent several years on assignment in

Riyadh in the hot and sandy centre of Saudi Arabia!

Part 3 describes an over two weeks' visit to Heather's Canadian relatives in Nanaimo, on Vancouver Island in Canada, in August and September 2018. It was a long outward journey, made even longer when forest fires prevented the seaplanes from operating across to Nanaimo from Vancouver due to poor visibility. For most of the visit we were in our favourite room in Nanaimo's Coast Bastion Hotel.

We had a very busy time in Nanaimo with Heather's relatives there, in particular her older brother Terry, who was nearing 90 years of age! He himself was very cheerful despite his age-related difficulties. The return journey was much more straightforward than the outward journey and went generally according to plan! Both the short Harbour Air seaplane flight and the Air Canada Long Haul flight were fine. Our arrival experience at Heathrow could have gone better, but then we had a smooth drive back home to Cirencester.

PART 1

Rhine River Cruise in June 2017

This one-week river cruise along the Rhine and Moselle Rivers in Germany was arranged with Riviera Travel – the UK based Tours and Cruises company. We flew from London Heathrow airport with a German airline – "German Wings" – to Cologne airport, departing at 2.25 pm (UK time) on 20th June 2017 and arriving at 5.10 pm (European time). We were taken by coach to where the cruise ship was moored on the bank of the Rhine River in Cologne, and at 6.20 pm we boarded the cruise ship – named the *MS Emily Brontë*. It was very hot in Cologne, about 32 degrees C. The planned itinerary is shown below. We would have some more time in Cologne at the end of the cruise.

Itinerary June 20 to 27th 2017

Day	Where
1 - June 20th	Travel to Cologne and embark onto *MS Emily Brontë*
2	Cochem
3	Trier
4	Bernkastel
5	Koblenz and Boppard
6	Rhine Gorge and Rudesheim
7	Cologne
8 - June 27th	Disembark and leave Cologne to travel home

Note:

Please note that - for each place visited in the later sections – the history of the place and the points of interest there are based on the descriptions in the leaflets provided to us before each visit by Riviera Travel. Also, the pictures shown are generally a mixture of our photographs and the freely available pictures on the internet.

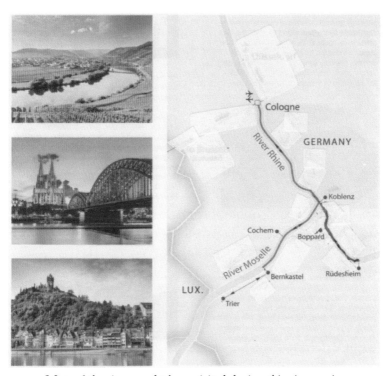

Map of the rivers and places visited during this river cruise

Typical view looking "aft" from the MS Emily Brontë

Typical view of the shoreline in June – cruising past castles and caravans!

Loading the vital beer supplies at one of our stops along the way!

2

Cologne – at the start

The first night on board was spent settling into our "cabin" and then making good use of the ship's refreshment facilities! We set off the next morning upstream along the Rhine towards the junction with the Moselle river and then along the Moselle to visit Cochem.

Cologne Cathedral (Kölner Dom) and the main railway line bridge across the Rhine

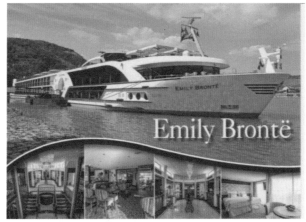

Riviera Travel's Postcard of the MS Emily Brontë – our cruise ship for this holiday

3

Cochem

<u>History of Cochem</u>

The earliest mentions of Cochem refer to settlements there in Celtic and Roman times. It was first mentioned in 886 AD as the "Villa Cuchema".

Today, it is a pleasure to wander around and explore Cochem with its narrow streets, steep twisting alleys, medieval town gates, churches and walls, the carefully restored half-timbered houses, and its historic old marketplace. There is a promenade along the Moselle River, with many benches available for a rest!

In the past, Cochem was at the centre of the Moselle wine trade, and there are ample opportunities to sample the local Riesling wines! Vineyards are all around, even on the rocky mound where the splendid Reichsburg Castle stands – Cochem's own castle. The castle has delicate pointed towers, battlements, oriel windows and huge walls, though we did not have the time to go there.

However, the castle has had an exciting past! First recorded in 1130 AD, it was occupied in 1151 AD by one King Konrad III, who declared it to be an Imperial Castle. It was overrun by the French King Louis XIV in 1688 AD and destroyed by his troops the following year. It then lay in ruins until 1868 AD, when it was reconstructed in its original style. Today, it is owned by the town of Cochem and specialises in serving hefty "medieval" meals with large stone mugs of Moselle wine!

<u>Riviera Travel's Points of Interest in Cochem</u>

A

Cochem Castle (Reichsburg Castle)

We did not have time to climb up to this renovated castle.

B

Historic Mustard Mill

Apparently, this old mustard mill has been renovated and has been producing mustard since 2001. We did not venture inside!

C

Chairlift to the Pinner Cross

We did take this chairlift to the mountain station at the top (and back). The station is more than 250 metres above sea level.

See photo below.

D

Historic Market Place

We went here during our sightseeing, and to pay a much-needed visit to the ATM!

See photo below.

*View over Cochem from the elevated Reichsburg Castle
(picture from internet)*

Heather stepping ashore from the MS Emily Brontë at Cochem

Probably, it is our MS Emily Brontë boat down on the river, as seen from on high

Travelling on the Chair Lift back down to Cochem

The historic Market Place in Cochem

Passing through a lock while going up the Moselle River,
after the stop at Cochem

4

Trier

History of Trier

Trier could well be the oldest city in Germany. An inscription (in Latin) on the side of a house in Trier market reads: "Thirteen hundred years before Rome, Trier stood. May it stand on and enjoy eternal peace." A legend says that it might have been founded by an Assyrian prince, but what is certain is that Trier was the capital of the large Roman province of Gallia Belgica, as well as the Roman prefecture of Gaul. It may then have had as many as 80,000 inhabitants.

The Roman Emperor Constantine lived in Trier in the 4th Century and greatly expanded the city. The city walls were strengthened with military towers and fortified gates. He ordered the building of a palace, an audience hall, and a massive imperial bathhouse – the largest north of the Alps. Constantine drove back an invasion by the Franks and captured two of their kings. Apparently, they were then fed to the hungry beasts in Trier's large amphitheatre!

The finest sight in Trier is the grey sandstone Porta Nigra, an immense fortified gate that towers above nearby medieval buildings. It is the largest and best-preserved Roman building north of the Alps. Originally there were four city gates, one on each side of the rectangular city. The Porta Nigra guarded the northern entry to the city and is the only one still standing today.

Other historical features of Trier include the medieval Hauptmarkt square, which contains many ancient buildings. The 2nd century Roman bridge across the Moselle River is the oldest bridge north of the Alps which is still being crossed by traffic.

Riviera Travel's Points of Interest in Trier

1   Basilica of Constantine (Aula Palatina)

2   High Cathedral of St. Peter (Hohe Domkirche St. Peter)

3   Porta Nigra (Latin for "Black Gate")

4   Church of Our Lady (Liebfrauenkirche)

5   Great Market (Hauptmarkt)

6   Roman Bridge (Römerbrücke)

7   Trier Amphitheatre

Our Visit to Trier

The *MS Emily Brontë* stopped at a place called Zell on the Moselle, where we got off the ship and onto a bus, which then drove us by road to Trier. It was even hotter there, about 35 to 38 degrees C! We were persuaded to walk around the central sights of the town for a few hours despite the heat! We tried to be in the shade whenever possible! It was a bit of a rushed hot tour, and we were quite glad to get back on the bus for the return drive to the ship. That night the ship was berthed at Bernkastel on the Moselle River.

Basilica of Constantine (or Aula Palatina) in Trier

Porta Nigra (or Black Gate) in Trier

Roman Bridge (or Römerbrücke) from Trier across the Moselle River

High Cathedral (or Hohe Domkirche) of St. Peter in Trier

Hauptmarkt (or Great Market Place) in Trier

Portal of the Church of Our Lady (or Liebfrauenkirche) in Trier

Façade of the Old Electoral Palace in Trier,
which now contains local government offices

5

Bernkastel

<u>History of Bernkastel</u>

The history of Bernkastel is said to be inseparable from wine! It is in the heart of the Moselle's beautiful wine lands. The Moselle's valley sides are covered with steep cultivated vineyards. There are no less than eighteen vineyards within the town limits.

Riesling is the main variety – the white aromatic grapes are used to make dry, semi-sweet, sweet, and sparkling white wines. Riesling is one of the world's most popular wine varieties and is usually included in the top three white wines, along with Chardonnay and Sauvignon Blanc. Smaller quantities of other less well-known varieties are also grown in and around Bernkastel.

The town has a charming cobbled market square surrounded by ornate, half-timbered houses with many dating from the 15th Century. Other well-known sights are the Spitzhäuschen (Pointed House) from the Middle Ages, the Renaissance Town Hall of 1608, the town gate (Graacher Tor), and several ancient fountains.

<u>Riviera Travel's Points of Interest in Bernkastel</u>

1   Landshut Castle (Burg Landshut)
     Originally built in 1277, the castle was destroyed by a fire in 1692.It is possible to climb up to the castle, but it is a strenuous climb! We did not go for this!

2   Spitzhäuschen (Pointed House)
     This little house with narrow gables was built in 1416 and is a popular photographic subject. See picture below.

3   Parish Church of St. Michael
     The imposing tower of this parish church is well over 600 years old, and contains many works of art. It was first

mentioned in records in 1177. The turret resembles a fortified tower. See picture below.

4   Market Square

      See description - above - and picture below.

5   Gate Graacher Tor (not seen)

6   Moselle Wine Museum (not seen)

Our Visit to Bernkastel

We had the morning to look around the town centre until returning to the ship which left at about 12.30 pm, and we could then have lunch on board. The ship went down the Moselle towards our next stop, which would be at Koblenz at the junction of the Moselle and the Rhine Rivers. That evening there was a very good "Bistro" style dinner on board followed by a musical quiz afterwards!

The Market Square in Bernkastel (picture from internet)

The Spitzhäuschen (Pointed House) in Bernkastel
(picture from internet)

The Tower of the Parish Church of St. Michael in Bernkastel
(picture from internet)

6

Koblenz

History of Koblenz

The waters of two important rivers – the Rhine and the Moselle - meet at Koblenz. The very name of Koblenz derives from the Latin word – *"confluentes"* – which means the merging of rivers. This age-old confluence takes place at the headland of the Deutsches Eck (or German Corner), which is also the site of a famous horseback statue of Wilhem I - the King of Prussia and the first German Emperor.

Founded by the Romans, and at the site of a bridge built in 55 BC by troops commanded by no less than Julius Caesar himself, Koblenz has had two thousand years of fascinating history. Over the centuries the town has been ruled by one Charles "the Bald", was captured by the Franks tribe, became a residence of the German Prince Electors, was conquered by the French, and fortified by the Prussians. It has received princes, kings, emperors, and presidents within its walls.

There are forest covered hillsides dominating the skyline with their lower slopes dotted with the attractive half-timbered buildings, which are typical of the Rhineland. Tiny streets, alleys, and passageways lead to small squares lined with traditional shops and cafes

There is an immense fortress built locally in three stages during the 19th century. Although difficult to see from the town itself across the Rhine, the fortress is high above the town and is in a dominating position. The fortress was built by Prussia as a key part of their regional fortification system to guard the Middle Rhine region. It successfully protected the area that had previously been attacked repeatedly by the French.

Riviera Travel's Points of Interest in Koblenz

1   Church Liebfrauenkirche

2   Church Florinskirche

3   Church St. Kastor

Other tourist attractions

4   Jesuit Church and City Hall

5   Fountain Schängelbrunnen

6   Shopping Street Lohrstrasse

7   Deutsches Eck (German Corner)

8   Ehrenbreitstein Fortress

<u>Our Visit to Koblenz</u>

We only had an hour or two to see around Koblenz before returning to the ship for lunch on board. Heather has noted in her diary that walking around Koblenz was "pretty boring"! It was still pretty hot too – Heather has noted a temperature there of 29 degrees C. We did however manage to visit a few of the Points of Interest on Riviera Travel's list.

A close-up view of the Fountain Schängelbrunnen in Koblenz, which intermittently and unexpectedly sprays out water!

*Deutsches Eck and the horseback statue of Kaiser Wilhelm I –
the first German Emperor*

The fountain is in the Town Hall square of Koblenz

*View of Koblenz and the merging of the Moselle –
the smaller river - and the Rhine*

The Florinskirche Church in Koblenz

7

Boppard

History of Boppard

Boppard's history also goes back to Celtic and Roman times. Today, it is a UNESCO World Heritage Site. One of the most attractive villages in the Rhineland, it is situated on one of the Rhine's most impressive and sweeping bends.

With a stone quayside lined with boats of all kinds, narrow cobbled old streets, half timbered houses and a fine main square, Boppard is every inch the classic picturesque Rhineland village. It is set within some of the best preserved Roman town walls in Germany – first built in the 4th Century and well used until the Middle Ages, when the town was expanded and gained new walls and towers.

Fine old buildings include the late Romanesque St. Severus Church, built in 1236. Then there is the Electoral Palace (Kurfurstliche Burg), or Old Castle, which today is Boppard's municipal museum, but in earlier times it was the symbol of the fight for local control.

Riviera Travel's Points of Interest in Boppard

1   Electoral Palace (Kurfürstliche Burg)

This castle was once one of the most important fortified complexes on the Middle Rhine. The structure now accommodates a regional Geography, Forest, and Woodland Museum.

2 & 3 Vierseenblick and Gedeonseck

The Vierseenblick look-out point above Boppard provides a wonderful view over four lakes. The Gedeonseck is a tavern also with a fabulous view over the largest twist in the Rhine River. A chairlift can take you up from Boppard and then back down.

4   Roman Fortifications

Extensive sections of Boppard's medieval defensive walls have been preserved.

5   St. Severus Church

This twin towered church dominates the view of the town from the Rhine. It dates back to the 13th Century and is Romanesque in style. The interior is colourful with interesting medieval frescoes.

6   Thonet Museum

A pioneer in the furniture industry, Thonet invented a technique in the mid-19th century that allowed rods of beechwood to be bent into delicate, curved shapes. By using this method, he went on to manufacture his famous coffee house furniture.

Boppard Market Place with St. Severus Church and a fountain

The Kurfürstliche Burg (Electoral Palace) is by the side of the Rhine in Boppard

Rüdesheim

History of Rüdesheim

Rüdesheim is another true Rhine "wine town". It is at the heart of the Riesling country, which is one of central Europe's finest wines, and the town is full of places to sample this refreshing drink! It is an idyllic place to stroll around and take in the charmingly crooked houses and equally crooked streets that lead down to the sweeping river, below wooded hillsides and terraced vineyards.

The Drosselgasse for one is a long narrow cobblestone lane in the centre of the old town. Originally built in the 15th Century to allow boat owners to move items from the river to their dwellings in the town, it is now home to wine taverns, open-air gardens, and restaurants that come alive with music during the summer months.

One can take an aerial ride on an unusual gondola lift with spectacular views across the river and the gorge. One can see the great statue of Germania that commemorates the Empire's Unification in 1871. Emperor Wilhelm II inaugurated this iconic monument that displays a relatively peaceful posture by holding a lowered sword.

Another delight in Rüdesheim is Siegfried's Mechanisches Musikkabinett, which is a mechanical music museum, with a large collection of antique musical instruments and musical boxes from all over the world, and many are still in good working order.

Riviera Travel's Points of Interest in Rudesheim

1   Niederwald Monument

This was constructed between 1871 and 1883. The total height is 38 metres and on top there is the 12.5 metre high statue of Germania, symbolising "the Guard of the Rhine". It is a tribute to the establishment of the German Empire immediately after the Franco-Prussian war. (Not visited)

2   Drosselgasse

This tiny street is at the heart of Rüdesheim's historic centre, and attracts visitors from near and wide. Live bands play vivacious music. We could well have walked past this!

3   Asbach Factory

Here, a typical German brandy (weinbrand) is made - a premium spirit, comparable to French brandy. Strangely though, this particular weinbrand is not made from German but from French grapes! Not visited.

Other tourist attractions: (but we had no time during our visit to seek these out!)

4   Adlerturm

5   Half-timbered house (Klunkhardshof)

6   St. Hildegard Abbey

7   Siegfried's Mechanisches Misikkabinett

Our visit to Rudesheim

The boat arrived at Rüdeheim at about 2 pm, and we had arranged to meet up with Pat Hoos, a cousin of Heather's, who lives in Germany and not too far from Rüdesheim. The boat moored at Mooring Point No. 19, and we met up with Pat quite soon after! Then we had a stroll together around the town centre of Rüdesheim. In the early evening Pat took us in her car to have dinner at the Schloss Johannesburg – a "fine dining" eating place in the buildings at the centre of a vineyard up in the hills above the town itself. There we managed to take a number of photos to commemorate this unusual family reunion event!

Typical eatery entrance in Rüdesheim

Vineyards and main buildings of Schloss Johannesburg above Rüdesheim (picture from internet)

Another tempting eatery in Rüdesheim

*Pat Hoos and Heather in the vineyard of Schloss Johannesburg,
near Rüdesheim*

Self and Heather in one of Pat's photos taken in Rüdesheim

Enjoying the food and the view from Schloss Johannesburg, near Rüdesheim

9

Cologne – at the end

History of Cologne

Construction of Cologne Cathedral (or Kölner Dom) was apparently started in 1248 AD and it was eventually finished in 1880 AD! Over 600 years later! It is the largest Gothic structure in the world. It was planned to be a grand structure, as a fitting place of worship for the Holy Roman Emperor, and to house the Shrine of the Three Kings – the relics of the three wise men who visited Jesus after his birth – they were named Caspar, Melchior, and Balthazar.

The Cathedral is Germany's most visited landmark and is a UNESCO World Heritage Site. It contains the most intricate stained glass in Europe, as well as the largest façade of any church in the world, thanks to its two enormous spires.

Around the Cathedral is Cologne's vibrant old town, well restored after World War II, with tree-lined squares, shops, and bars. Some of the bars even brew their own traditional beer, especially the Kölsch variety. Karl Marx is said to have remarked that his revolution couldn't work in Cologne, as the bosses drank in the same bars as their workers!

Founded in 38 BC by a Germanic tribe, Cologne later became a Roman settlement in 50 AD. During the Middle Ages it flourished on an important European east-west trade route, and it became one of the largest cities north of the Alps in medieval times. Many fine medieval churches, houses and city gates remain today.

<u>Riviera Travel's Points of Interest in Cologne</u>

1   Cologne Cathedral (Kölner Dom)

2   Town Hall

3   The Twelve Great Romanesque Churches

   All these churches except one were badly damaged during World War II and rebuilding them took until 1985.

Other tourist attractions

4   Old Town (Altstadt)

5   Museum Ludwig

6   Chocolate Museum

<u>Our Visit to and Departure from Cologne at the end of this holiday</u>

During the next morning, the ship travelled down the Rhine from Rüdesheim to Cologne, which was our last stop on this river cruise. That afternoon we spent looking around Cologne with most of the time being spent finding and viewing the famous Cologne Cathedral – see the pictures below. That evening we had the Last Night Dinner (or Captain's Dinner!) on board and were getting ready to disembark early the next morning. We were told to be out of our cabin by 9 AM!

   Soon after 10 AM we left the *MS Emily Brontë* to catch the German Wings flight, which left Cologne airport at about 13.30 pm to arrive at London Heathrow Terminal 2 at about 2 pm (UK time). We then managed to get back home to Cirencester at about 4.30 pm that afternoon.

View of Cologne Cathedral and the shoreline of the river Rhine

A view inside Cologne Cathedral

A selection of photos of the famous Cologne Cathedral from different viewpoints

Impressive statue of one of the German Kaisers by a bridge in Cologne

36

PART 2

United Arab Emirates (UAE) in November 2017

1

Itinerary

November 17th to 25th 2017

(Note: Our 40th Wedding Anniversary was on November 22nd, 2017)

This one week outing to the UAE (United Arab Emirates) in the Middle East, in November 2017, was booked with the UK office of RSD Travel, a multi-national European travel organisation. Travel Insurance was arranged by RSD with HanseMerkur Travel Insurance of Germany for a very reasonable cost.

Day	Where
1 – November 17th	Drive from Cirencester to stay overnight at the Holiday Inn Hotel, near London Gatwick Airport
2 – November 18th	Travel by Air to Abu Dhabi via Istanbul, Turkey
3 – November 19th	Abu Dhabi
4 – November 20th	Dubai
5 – November 21st	Dubai
6 – November 22nd	Ajman – on our 40th Wedding Anniversary!
7 – November 23rd	Ajman
8 – November 24th	Depart hotel for Overnight flights to London Gatwick, via Istanbul

9 – November 25th   Arrive home in Cirencester at about 2.30pm

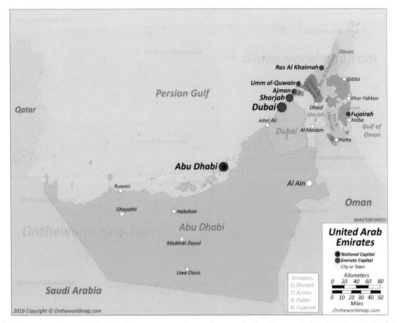

There are Seven UAE Emirates altogether, of which we visited Abu Dhabi, Dubai and Ajman

2

Outward Travel to Abu Dhabi

The outward journey from the UK to Abu Dhabi was somewhat complicated! Due to the relatively early departure time of 10:15 a.m. from London Gatwick airport, we spent the night before take-off at a hotel on the edge of the airport. We chose the Holiday Inn there and drove by car from Cirencester, leaving at about 11:30 a.m. to arrive at the hotel at about 3 p.m. The hotel was perfectly adequate, and we were able to have a reasonably normal night's sleep and breakfast before driving to an airport car park and then going by bus to the terminal serving Turkish Airlines.

Our Turkish Airlines flight (TK 1982) was fine and arrived in Istanbul's Ataturk International Airport on schedule at about 17:05 p.m. (local time). (Note - Istanbul's Atatürk International Airport used to be the busiest of Turkey's major airports. It was fully replaced by the new Istanbul Airport in October 2018.)

There was then plenty of time to transfer onto the next flight (TK 868 departing at 19:40 p.m.) to take us from Istanbul to Abu Dhabi. This flight had to follow quite a hazardous route after leaving Turkey, to go down above the border between Iran and Iraq to the Arabian (or Persian) Gulf and then down past Kuwait, Bahrain and Qatar to arrive at Abu Dhabi in the United Arab Emirates. We were quite near Saudi Arabia towards the end of this flight which brought back memories for us of our assignment there long, long ago in the late 1970s! The flames of the gas flares in the many oil fields along the route were still burning bright!

We landed at Abu Dhabi soon after 1:00 a.m. in the morning of the next day (November 19th) and were bussed to the hotel to arrive there and into our room at about 2:40 a.m.! The hotel was the 5 Star Hotel Grand Millennium Al Wahda. We eventually staggered into bed at about 3:00 a.m.!

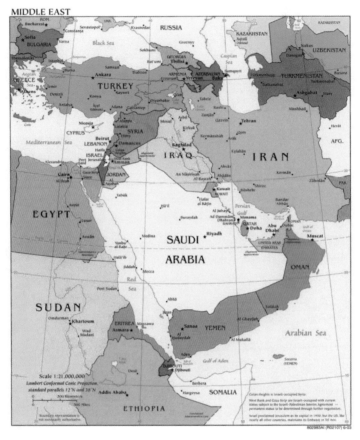

Map of the Middle East showing Saudi Arabia and the United Arab Emirates

3

Abu Dhabi

Abu Dhabi is the capital city of the United Arab Emirates (UAE), and it lies slightly off the mainland on an island in the waters of the Persian (or Arabian) Gulf. The UAE's focus on oil exports and commerce is reflected by the skyline of modern towers and shopping centres such as the Abu Dhabi and Marina Malls. Beneath white-marble domes, the vast Sheikh Zayed Grand Mosque features an immense Persian carpet, crystal chandeliers and the capacity for 41,000 worshipers!

Summary of Our Guide's Points of Interest in Abu Dhabi

(Our English-Speaking Guide was a Cypriot Lady, whose name was Ozlem Denez)

Sheikh Zayed Mosque – This was the most impressive place we visited.

Ferrari World

Yas Island Boat Tour

Boat Tour – Abu Dhabi Skyline - Dinner and Soft Drinks included

Our Hotel was the Luxury 5-star Grand Millennium Al Wahda, Abu Dhabi

RSD's picture and description of this hotel (see below)

*Our Hotel in Abu Dhabi was next to the Al Wahda Mall –
but we had no time to visit this!*

Hotel Description - based on the RSD leaflets

Location: This hotel is centrally located in Abu Dhabi, the capital of the United Arab Emirates, and is linked with the elegant Al Wahda Mall where you can shop to your heart's content at 350 brand outlets.

It's only a 15-minute drive to the famous Abu Dhabi Corniche beach promenade and a mere 3 kilometres from the Al Hosn Palace built in 1793, making it Abu Dhabi's oldest building!

Features: This luxury hotel with maximum comfort and elegance has three different restaurants where you can enjoy authentic Italian, International, Asian and local cuisine as well as various snacks. The lobby lounge offers tea, coffee and various juices as well as delicious pastries. You can relax in the hotel spa where you can be pampered by various treatments and massages. Another highlight is the hotel's roof terrace featuring a swimming pool and the Al Wahda Health Club.

Accommodation: All 844 rooms feature a flat-screen TV, direct-dial telephone, Wi-Fi, a spacious seating area, minibar (subject to charge), free tea and coffee making facilities, a safe and air-conditioning. The spacious bathrooms feature a WC, a separate bath and a shower as well as a hairdryer.

RSD's "Explorer" Excursion Package

While booking, we had opted for this extra cost item, which had seemed a good offer at a reasonable price! As "Rowsie" explains in a later chapter, some of these extra excursions were a bit of a con, and just amounted to looking out of the bus window as we drove through somewhere! Anyway, here are the four elements of this Explorer Excursion Package, mostly in Abu Dhabi, and based on the descriptions in the RSD leaflets.

Abu Dhabi Tour – On this tour, you will become better acquainted with Abu Dhabi, the capital of the UAE. You will see the Heritage Village and the Emirates Palace as well as the Sheikh Zayed Mosque, the largest mosque in the Emirates.

Abu Dhabi Boat Trip including dinner – A special evening event on board a traditional "Dhow" and enjoying the illuminated skyline of Abu Dhabi. On-board catering will be provided while you cruise along the coast.

Dubai Sightseeing Tour – A short boat trip across the Dubai Creek will bring you to the spice market and the Gold Souk. This is followed by a visit to the "Madinat Jumeirah", which was built in the style of old Arabian palaces and features an extensive channel of waterways. Further stops are the Al Fahidi Fort housing the Dubai Museum (incl. admission), the Dubai Mall as well as the world's tallest building – the "Burj Khalifa".

Boat Trip around Yas Island – The island is best known for its Formula One motor racing circuit, the "Yas Marina Circuit" and the Ferrari World theme park. From there our tour takes you to "Saadiyat Island". Cultural institutions such as the Louvre Abu Dhabi and the Guggenheim Museum are due to open here soon. (But they were not yet open on our visit!)

Our Visit to Abu Dhabi

We really only had the one day in Abu Dhabi, as we arrived in the hotel at 2:40 a.m. in the early morning of Sunday, November 19th, and departed from the hotel at 9:30 a.m. on the Monday morning! A pity as we were staying at a very luxurious 5 Star hotel!

We were up at about 6:00 a.m. to make the most of this first day. After breakfast, we were told about our guide's plans for the rest of the week. Then it was a pretty full day doing the planned sightseeing outings in Abu Dhabi, as outlined above. The best visit was to the Sheikh Zayed Mosque (see below). Next in order of interest was the Ferrari World theme park, but the boat trips, and refreshments on one of the boats, were less interesting! We probably turned in fairly early after our late arrival the night before!

Hotel swimming pool on the topmost roof terrace

View over Abu Dhabi city from a window by our hotel's swimming pool

Sheikh Zayed Mosque in Abu Dhabi – as shown on a postcard

Inside the Sheikh Zayed Mosque in Abu Dhabi

Heather in suitable mosque viewing attire!

Other tourists visiting the Sheikh Zayed Mosque

Self in one of the outside courtyards within the mosque

An impressive chandelier inside the mosque

Later in a mall: Self not about to buy any Camel Milk Ice Cream!

An actual Ferrari racing car inside the Ferrari World theme park

Expensive watches were for sale at the Ferrari World theme park
(But check out the AED (the UAE Dirham) exchange rate!)

Entrance to the Ferrari World theme park.

*A young – probably Japanese –
tourist at the Ferrari World theme park.*

4

Dubai

Dubai is a city and an emirate in the United Arab Emirates known for its luxury shopping, ultramodern architecture, and "lively" nightlife. Burj Khalifa, an 830m-tall tower, dominates the skyscraper-filled skyline. At its foot lie the Dubai Fountains, with jets and lights at night choreographed to music. On artificial islands just offshore lies Atlantis, The Palm, a resort with water and marine-animal parks.

Camels and Skyscrapers are supposed to be features of Dubai!
(but we did not actually see any real live camels in downtown Dubai!)

In the background is the Burj Al Arab Hotel in Dubai
(from a picture postcard)

The Ultra-Luxurious Burj Al Arab Hotel – we did not stay there!

<u>Summary of our Guide's Points of Interest in Dubai</u>

On Monday November 20th

    Dubai Mall

    Dubai Heritage Museum

    Souks (Local Markets)

    (At extra cost was a Dhow Dinner Cruise in the Dubai Marina, but not for us!)

On Tuesday November 21st

    Dubai Sightseeing

    Palm Island (for everybody)

    Cultural Art Centre

    (At extra cost was a trip to Dubai By Night – Burj Khalifa and Burj Al Arab Hotel –   but not for us!)

On Wednesday November 22nd

    Shopping (!)

    Sharjah Sightseeing

    Transfer to Ajman

<u>Our Hotel in Dubai was the Luxury 4-star TIME Grand Plaza Hotel</u>

RSD's Description and Picture of this hotel in Dubai:

<u>Location:</u> This comfortable 4-star hotel was built in 2010 and is in the vicinity of numerous sights such as the Burj Khalifa and the Dubai Mall.

<u>Features:</u> Look forward to a spacious reception area with a lobby bathed in light and perfect for relaxing. Featuring high-quality furnishings, the 232 spacious rooms offer maximum comfort. Apart from a cosy café, you can also enjoy international cuisine and local dishes in the hotel restaurant. A spa is available for relaxation as well as a very well-equipped gym. Another highlight is the heated pool with a pool bar on the roof terrace.

<u>Accommodation:</u> The comfortable rooms feature a bath or shower, WC, hairdryer, slippers, bathrobes, tea and coffee making facilities, telephone, Wi-Fi (subject to charge), sat TV, minibar (subject to charge), safe and air-conditioning.

Our Luxury 4-star hotel: The TIME Grand Plaza Hotel in Dubai

The "Golden Fork" fish restaurant near the hotel –
where we had dinner one night in Dubai! (picture from internet)

Heather admiring the views in the centre of Dubai

The Burj Khalifa tower by day and by night

Various sights around the Dubai Malls –
Heather's Canadian relatives are big fans of their local Tim Hortons for coffees!

Spacious walkways in the Dubai malls

There were boat rides for tourists around the waterways of Dubai

A picture from one of the RSD brochures!

Entrance to a colourful souk (or market) – not sure what was for sale!

We were able to buy this carpet in Dubai!

Label on our carpet – with Heather's signature on it to ensure that we received the same one! (It was safely delivered to us after we had returned home to the UK)

Self on tour in Dubai

One of the malls had impressive and very large aquariums

I don't think the taps etc. were actually gold plated, but they looked good!

A photo opportunity when the bus stopped, and we went outside

Heather looking away from the impressive view!

Dubai central square at night – as seen from a restaurant's upper floor

The fountains "danced" up and down to the music to accompany our dinner!

5

Ajman

Ajman is the capital city of the Emirate of Ajman in the United Arab Emirates. It is the fifth-largest city in the UAE after Dubai, Abu Dhabi, Sharjah and Al Ain. Located on the Persian Gulf, Ajman is surrounded by the territory of the larger emirate of Sharjah.

Summary of the Guide's Points of Interest in Ajman

On Thursday November 23rd

Desert Safari in Ajman – we booked (and paid extra for this experience!) – see later

On Friday November 24th

At much extra cost was a Coach Tour to Oman – but not for us!

Our Hotel – the Luxury 5-star Ajman Palace, Ajman

Hotel Description – based on RSD leaflets

Location: Only 30 minutes' drive away from the vibrant city of Dubai, this luxurious hotel is right on the sunny coast of the Ajman Emirate, offering a breathtakingly white sandy beach. Enjoy the real Arab traditions as well as its famous hospitality.

Facilities: Your resort is distinguished by its modern architecture and offers its guests the epitome of elegance. The hotel offers a range of first-class restaurants and culinary delicacies. Some of the restaurants and lounges offer outdoor seating with views of the Persian Gulf. And guests seeking relaxation will be thrilled with the beautiful long sandy beach.

Accommodation: Each of the bedrooms in the hotel offers a fantastic view of the sea or the city, and has modern and elegant furnishings, including a flat-screen TV, a minibar (subject to charge), free tea and coffee-making facilities, a safe and air-conditioning. Bathrooms feature a luxurious design and have a shower as well as a separate bath, and hairdryer.

Desert Safari in Ajman

One of the brochures provided the following picture and enthusiastic description of this – the only real "add on" that we invested in – as a reminder of our years in Riyadh, in the middle of Saudi Arabia - many moons ago!

"DESERT SAFARI

Experience the thrill of a lifetime with a roller-coaster ride in the sand dunes. Our desert safari gives you an opportunity to see the golden sand dunes of Arabia in 4-wheel vehicles. While on the journey, you will stop on the highest sand dune to view the beautiful sunset and to refresh yourself with a mineral water.

Continue the drive to an authentic Bedouin campsite right in the heart of the desert, where henna design, local dresses, soft drinks, water, tea, or coffee are available for your enjoyment.

Try your hands on some camel rides and get a taste of the Hubbly Bubbly (water pipe), available in different flavours. Adding to the atmosphere of the night, an enchanting belly dancer performs a fascinating dance to the rhythm of Arabic music. To top it all, a delicious barbeque buffet dinner is served under the stars."

Typical of our rather "hairy" drives through the sand dunes of Ajman

Note:

Needless to say, we did <u>not</u> indulge in the camel rides, nor the Hubbly Bubbly experience, nor the application onto our bodies of colourful henna designs (body and/or hair dyes!). But we did enjoy the Desert Drive and the food in the Bedouin campsite accompanied by Arabic music – but I do not remember a belly-dancer!

We had a relaxing breakfast in the hotel's outside restaurant before the afternoon's Desert Safari excitement!

The Hotel's beach frontage faced onto the Gulf waters to the west

Even our 4X4 SUVs had trouble in the deep sand!

Observing the sunset during our Desert Safari

Well – my red shorts added even more colour to the sunset!

At the Bedouin Camp in the Ajman desert before supper

Arabic musicians entertained us from a raised stage
(But there were no belly dancers that I remember!)

Shopping!

As it was nearly the end of this brief visit to the United Arab Emirates, we had to inspect the local shopping opportunities, such as are shown on the following photos!

The Gold Souk was a magnet for Heather – but we were not sure about those Gold Rates! What are those Gold Rates in Pounds Sterling or US dollars!

A couple of "Department Store" type shops within walking distance of our Ajman hotel

Even in the Middle East in late November, you cannot escape Christmas!

6

Return Travel to the UK

We had another complicated journey to return back to the UK. We had to check out from our room at the Ajman Palace Hotel by 12.00 noon, which we managed to achieve. We then had a free afternoon and early evening before being picked up at about 8:30 p.m. by the bus taking us to Abu Dhabi Airport for the return flight to Istanbul and then on to London Gatwick Airport.

It would have been good to have spent the afternoon on the beach, but not very practical to do that as our bags and gear were all packed up and stored with the reception people! So, we went on a walkabout to the local shopping area called Centrepoint, which was a fairly lengthy walk along the sea front. Small last-minute items were the order of the day to be fitted into our "carry on" bags!

We joined the rest of the group for an evening meal in the hotel restaurant at 6:30 p.m. and the bus for the airport duly left at about 8:40 p.m. It was a long drive by road to Abu Dhabi Airport and it was not until about 11:40 p.m. that we reached it. There we checked in for the Turkish Airlines flight to Istanbul, which duly took off at 2:45 a.m. – in the middle of the night! We reached Istanbul at about 6:30 a.m. in the early morning – not much sleep having been achieved. The second return flight to London Gatwick left Istanbul just after 8:00 a.m. and we eventually landed at London Gatwick at about 9:20 a.m. – not feeling very bright!

There, we were reunited with our car and drove back to Cirencester – but due to the M4 being closed between junctions 12 and 13 – we had to make a large diversion. We arrived back at the house at about 2:15 p.m. (UK time) – and goodness knows how long the return journey had taken! There was the expected pile of mail awaiting us, and my diary recorded that the "First Christmas Card" had come while we were away! It then took us several nights to catch up with lost sleep.

7

Article by Rowsie

After we had returned home to Cirencester, we came across this online article by a lady called Rowsie – a "Silver Traveller" – just like us! She and her sister had evidently been on a very similar holiday to ours with RSD to the UAE in May 2017, which would have been a hotter month than ours was in November 2017. So, it seemed to be a good idea to include her article – see below!

Rowsie's Title was "Abu Dhabi and Dubai (and Ajman too!)"

- By Silver Traveller	*Rowsie*
- Visit Date	May 2017
- Travelled With	Adult sister

Anyone who has read my past reviews might recall that I have travelled with RSD before and after my last experience my sister and I decided we probably would not travel with them again. However, we were seduced by the offer that popped into my mailbox "8 days in Abu Dhabi and Dubai from £299"

RSD is a company that do very cheap trips and make their money by offering "add ons" (which do bring the cost of the holiday up quite a bit). In the past, my sister and I have declined these "add ons" and when the rest of the group were being herded into cavernous touristy restaurants for lunch or dinner, we could be found in a bistro nearby or just on the beach with a supermarket picnic. I have been to Dubai before but have never been to Abu Dhabi and the price was so tempting that we went ahead and booked. (Although when we chose our dates, the price was nowhere near £299!)

However, it was still cheap, and our flight was good. Turkish Airways to Istanbul then another Turkish Airways flight to Dubai. We were impressed with Turkish Airways, nice staff, good leg room and good food. We arrived at midnight and had a 2-hour drive to our first hotel, The Grand Millennium Al Wahda in Abu Dhabi. Our room was nice, and I have to say that RSD do always seem to use wonderful hotels. We were told to meet our guide at 11 a.m. the next morning.

At that meeting our guide, Hatice (a Cypriot lady) was very friendly and welcoming. The "add ons" this time were a £110 package which included: an Abu Dhabi Tour, an Abu Dhabi boat trip and dinner, a Dubai sightseeing tour and a boat trip around Yas Island. As I said we have never bought these packages before, but this sounded good value for £110 so we bought this. Over the next few days, it became apparent that this was a little bit of a con as the sightseeing tours were literally just driving through the towns en route to our hotels!

Our first trip covered by the package was to Yas Island (where the Formula 1 takes place). We had a boat trip down the river and saw Ferrari World and the Formula 1 venue from afar. Then we went to the very impressive Sheik Zayed Mosque – the largest mosque in the Emirates. Hatice had told us that we had to cover up completely to visit. I had heard that you could hire gowns to wear but she said that they didn't do this anymore. So, we were all wearing our English winter clothes and were melting in the 40 degrees heat! The mosque was very beautiful and well worth the visit, but it seems that they still do offer the lightweight gowns as lots of people were wearing them! After we had lost a few pounds by wandering around in our coats and thick trousers it was back on the coach for the "city tour" that was, in fact, just the route back to our hotel. The next part of our package was a dinner cruise on a large dhow that evening. That was very nice although we held the boat up for 30 minutes. This was because Hatice spent ages collecting money from people for additional trips she had offered. She spent too long berating people who had changed their minds about the trips and at one point she almost blackmailed some poor women into paying for an extra excursion! The pretty Cypriot lady had a rather nasty temper! She was also very rude to our driver who took a wrong turn at one point. However, despite the glares from the other passengers as we boarded the dhow, the buffet was nice, the views were lovely, and it was a pleasant evening. (You could also buy alcohol on board which is not something you can do easily in the UAE).

The next day we were off to Dubai. Hatice had recovered and was very informative en route. She had a tendency to make the UAE sound like a Utopia but I am not sure about that. She said there were only 4 crimes last year in Abu Dhabi. Really? I wondered if a lot of crimes just don't get reported, especially crimes against women, like wife beating and abuse of servants. It would be interesting to find out more about that.

Obviously, on arrival in Dubai we were too early to check into our hotel, so our "Dubai City Tour" consisted of being dropped at the Dubai Mall for 2 hours. We weren't interested in shopping, so we used our time to go up the Burj Khalifa, the tallest building in the world. We went up to the 125th and 124th floors and saw the wonderful views. A must do place! Fabulous! Back down in the Mall we still had time to see the outside of the Aquarium (the most gigantic tank full of sharks, stingrays etc and even some divers!), the impressive waterfall with statues of divers and then just had time to see the fountains outside the Mall dance to music which they do every 15 minutes. Back on our City Tour we went to the Dubai Museum (OK, but not that impressive) and then went across the river to the old quarter on a small ferry boat (lovely, but very short ride). Then despite the fact that we were all wilting in the heat we were given far too much time in the textile souk, the spice souk, and the gold souk. Everyone was just wanting to get to the hotel by then and no one had any enthusiasm for the colourful souks. So really our £110 package, with the exception of the mosque and the river cruises, was just a way to keep us entertained before our hotels were ready!

Finally, we got to our Dubai hotel, the 4-star City Seasons Towers. Hatice had not been very enthusiastic about this hotel, but we liked it. The staff were lovely, and the only downside was the very small swimming pool. Hatice had advised us that there was another "complimentary" trip the next day. Exhausted from being herded around in a group we declined, especially when we heard it was to include a carpet factory visit! Hatice was very annoyed at us for declining to go and accused us of "not believing in RSD's policies" (whatever that means!). She then proceeded to ignore us for the rest of the week! We only found out our departure times etc. from other guests! In retrospect we regret giving her a tip (albeit a small one) as she didn't even say goodbye to us on the last day!

Anyway, with time to ourselves in Dubai we had a great day. We bought a Metro All Day ticket (22 Dirham, about £4) and travelled all round Dubai on the Metro, Tram, Bus, and Monorail. We visited the Atlantis Palm Hotel, which is quite spectacular, went to the Burj Al Arab building (but hadn't booked so couldn't go up it) which looks spectacular and then went back to the Dubai Mall to have dinner outside by the fountains which were beautifully lit up at night. We had a magical evening sitting in the shadow of the Burj Khalifa.

The next day we were off to Ajman for 2 ½ days. Hatice said (not directly to us as she was ignoring us, but to the coach in general) that we would have some "interesting" trips en route. This turned out to be a visit to a jewellery factory and a visit to a leather factory. We had 2 hours at each venue, and no one was really interested in either and there was nowhere to sit whilst we waited for the few people who did buy. We then drove through Sharjah which is the most restricted state in the UAE and then on to Ajman (another of the 7 states that make up the UAE). At first sight of our hotel in Ajman (The Ajman Fairmont) we all bucked up considerably. A beautiful hotel set right on the beach. All rooms have balconies, and the view is incredible. Everyone rushed off to get their swimsuits on, oblivious to the fact that Hatice had made a hasty retreat, clutching her tips envelope and without a farewell to anyone!

Our final 2 ½ days were wonderful. The hotel had a Caribbean beach bar, a more sophisticated open-air bar on the 1st floor and three restaurants to choose from. The staff were all lovely and helpful. We basked on the beach and swam in the beautifully warm Persian Gulf. RSD do get some things right!

So, if you get an offer you can't refuse from RSD, bear in mind that their hotel choices are brilliant, their prices are cheap, but be prepared for the pushy guides and the factory visits!

Unfortunately, our flight home was a nightmare as we missed the connecting flight in Istanbul. We arrived home 5 hours late, but these things happen, and we were still in the afterglow of the relaxing time we had spent in Ajman.

Lastly, a few pointers for people travelling to the UAE:

- Obviously respect the Islamic faith. Other than the Mosque visit, we did not have to cover up but walking around the cities in short shorts and skimpy tops isn't very respectful.

- Definitely don't sunbathe topless (or are all of us *Silver Travellers* past that now anyway?)

- Be prepared, if you are a woman, to be treated like a second-class citizen. We were ignored in bars and restaurants whilst men coming in after us were rushed through to the best tables.

- Alcohol is only available in some hotels and a few bars. You can't buy it in supermarkets and most small restaurants don't have it. It is also expensive when you can get it. If this is a problem, check before you go that your hotel serves it.

- In Abu Dhabi and Dubai there was a "bed tax" of 30 Dirhams per room in each hotel.

- In Ajman there was no bed tax but there was 10% service on everything and a 20% Tourist tax!

PART 3

Canada in August – September 2018

1

Outward Journey on

Tuesday August 21st 2018

Departed London Heathrow Terminal 2 at 2:10 p.m. – Arrived Vancouver Airport 3:35 p.m.

As we had done on this outward journey quite a few times before, the plan was then to take a taxi to the Seaplane Terminal (a few miles from the main Vancouver airport) and to catch the 5:30 p.m. Harbour Air seaplane across the channel to Nanaimo on Vancouver Island where Heather's brother Terry and his wife Ann and their many Canadian relatives live.

However, it was a hot August that year! and there were many forest fires in the area, which were emitting so much smoke that the seaplanes were not flying due to the poor visibility!

There was the fall-back alternative, thank goodness, of crossing the channel by ferry, but that involved another taxi ride and a long wait for the next ferry, which of course took much longer than the seaplane! Terry and his wife Ann kindly met us at the ferry terminal in Nanaimo to take us to our hotel – the excellent Coast Bastion Hotel in the centre of Nanaimo. We eventually checked in there at 9:45 p.m. their time.

One further difficulty on this outward journey was that we wanted to be in the room we have used and liked before (Room 809).

However, unknown to us at the time, the Canadian Prime Minister and his reshuffled cabinet were then holding a series of meetings (called a "Retreat") in Nanaimo and the room we liked was not yet available for us. So, we had to stay in a poorer room for our first two nights, until our preferred room became available, presumably after all those important Canadian politicians had left!

Our favourite room (Room 809) –
But we had to wait a couple of days to move in!

The wonderful view over Nanaimo Harbour
from the window of "Our Room" Room 809!

2

Wedding in Dawson Creek

A few weeks before we arrived in Canada, a family wedding with a difference had taken place in Dawson Creek in northern British Columbia, near the border with Alberta. For those less knowledgeable about the geography of Western Canada, Dawson Creek is some 800 miles by road to the north of Nanaimo or Vancouver, which means a long drive even using the major highways. But several family members from Nanaimo did make this journey to attend this family wedding!

So, Terry's grandson Ryan Kloosterboer married his bride Anna on or about August 5th 2018 at Dawson Creek in a picturesque rural style wedding, as illustrated in the following photos, some of which were taken by myself from a video film (cleverly playing on a continuous loop) being shown at Alison and Keith Kloosterboer's house at the "Super Casual" garden party they hosted later on, which we were able to attend after we arrived in Nanaimo!

Dawson Creek is at "Mile Zero" of the Alaska Highway, which then runs all the way from there to Alaska! (picture from internet)

Ryan being supported by three male supporters and ready for anything!

Ryan and a friend with bales of harvested crops

Ryan and Anna in happy modes!

Another photo of the happy couple!

Another photo of the bride and groom!

But don't pull too hard on those wooden poles!

Lindsay, Andy and their family in the fields

Anna, Ryan, Lindsay and Sara that evening

It looks like a picnic tea for Annika, Sara and baby Theo

Alison and Keith possibly at a roadside café en route to or from Dawson Creek

3

Super Casual Food and Fun Party

To celebrate Ryan and Anna's earlier wedding in Dawson Creek, Alison and Keith – Ryan's parents – hosted a "Super Casual Food and Fun Party" on a Saturday in the late afternoon and evening at their house in Nanaimo with its large garden. There were many people there – approximately 40 in number and at least 2 dogs! We did not know everyone except immediate family, but I will leave it to the following pictures to better illustrate this "fun" event. I did come across a video screen (showing pictures of the wedding) inside the house and was able to snap some of the pictures of the wedding which had happened up in Dawson Creek some weeks earlier. Those pictures were included in the previous chapter.

Terry and Ann were among the early arrivals!
It looks like a "playhouse" for any toddlers behind them!

View from the outside balcony as people began to arrive

Another view of other party goers soon after arrival

Anna is "in the pink" and enjoying the party!

Self, Heather, Terry (seated on chairs)
Chris and Bobbi are standing behind Terry

Lindsay and her latest baby!

Peter and Ann Kloosterboer are Ryan's grandparents

Chris, Bobbi, Anna and Ryan must be sharing a subtle joke?

Anna, Ryan, Annika and Sara seated in a row!

Self, Heather, Terry, Chris and Bobbi, as it began to get darker

It looks like about 40 heads and 2 dogs in this "Team Photograph"

Around the campfire – I do not remember any singing though!

4

A Walk in a Big Park

A distant cousin of Heather's (Kevin Dyck) and his partner (Sandy) who live in Edmonton, Alberta, travelled down to Nanaimo for a long weekend visit to meet up with Kevin's distant cousins from the UK and Nanaimo. We picked them up at the airport and drove them back to the Coast Bastion hotel, where they were also staying. On one of the days during their visit, the four of us drove up to the north of Nanaimo for a tour of the area in and around the town of Qualicum Beach. After lunch at Qualicum Beach, we went into the MacMillan Provincial Park, better known to locals by its former name – Cathedral Grove. In this coastal forest are giant Douglas Fir trees and groves of ancient Western Red Cedar trees near the Cameron Lake. There had been a severe storm there in 1997 which had toppled hundreds of these huge trees, and many were still lying on the ground. We parked the car in an official parking area and set off through the well signposted trails!

Unfortunately, when we returned to the parking area, Heather discovered that she had lost her (very expensive!) Tiffany sunglasses. Both Heather and Kevin retraced our steps around the park searching for the sunglasses, but without success. There were no officials in the park to whom Heather could report her loss. On returning to the UK, we submitted a claim to the travel insurance company we had used, and they did eventually pay up an amount, but not as much as Heather had paid to buy those Tiffany sunglasses, only one year before. It is probably a good idea to take out travel insurance for such trips abroad, but it's even better not to lose anything if possible!

Sandy and Heather near the start of the trail

Strange how some parts of the tree roots are so far above the ground

Heather and some large fallen trees

Self and Heather and more fallen trees!

Perhaps a stricken giant Douglas Fir tree was behind us

*This information plaque about the Douglas Fir was
by the side of the trail*

After the walk - Heather, Kevin and Sandy in Terry and Ann's Garden

That evening was spent in studying family history documents

Looks like it's time for the supper break!

5

Cannon Firing Ceremony

Just outside our Coast Bastion Hotel were this pair of old cannons on the waterfront right by the old Bastion Building – originally constructed as a defensive building, apparently in the 1850s. During the summer months at noon there is a ceremonial cannon firing event, accompanied by a bagpiper (in his kilt!) playing his strange Scottish musical instrument! How could we resist watching this one day, when we had some free time at about noon and to witness this historical event!

Cannons and the piper in his kilt by the Bastion on the Nanaimo waterfront

Another view of the cannons and the piper

The brave piper is covering his sensitive ears!

Viewed against a different background

The piper is carefully approaching the cannons after the firing!

6

Boat Trip and Pub Afterwards

For a Saturday afternoon treat, Keith and Alison took us four visitors (We two, and Kevin and Sandy) for an exciting boat trip around Nanaimo harbour, which showed us the large extent of this natural harbour and its waters, from the relatively built-up commercial shipping area around the town of Nanaimo itself to the relatively wild and wooded areas away from the town.

Getting the boat off the trailer and into the water

From the left – Heather, Kevin, Keith (at the controls), Sandy and Alison

Alison and Sandy in discussion and in their "shades"

View looking "aft" with the boat travelling at speed!

Keith was at the controls and the "steering wheel"

Self, Heather, and Kevin admiring the watery views

During one of our Nanaimo visits, we bought a couple of table matts – one is pictured above. This shows the general geography of the area around Nanaimo and its harbour and nearby islands.
Our boat trip with Keith must have been along the waterways between Gabriola Island and the mainland around Nanaimo.

That evening we retired to a very noisy and merry Irish Pub for evening refreshments!

*Three pictures of Carlos O'Bryan's Irish Pub within
the Nanaimo Harbour marina*

7

Visits with Relatives

At a Big Sunday "Brunch" in the Modern Café in downtown Nanaimo

A group of the Watkins "clan" –
Chris, Alison, Heather and Terry with Ann behind them

Self, Annika, Sara and Heather at Sara & Annika's residence

*Self and the Galloway family at Terry and Ann's house
on our last full day in Nanaimo*

Self, Keith, Heather and Terry around the table

Heather, Terry, Peter & Ann K and Andy plus son at the table!

The "Team Photograph" at Terry & Ann's house
Peter & Ann K, Keith & Alison, Self & Heather, Andy & Terry
On the floor: Sara and Lindsay and the 2 small Galloways

A favourite local eatery is the White Spot restaurant in Nanaimo

The Chapters Coffee Shop is in a shopping centre in Nanaimo

Inside the Longwood Station pub in Nanaimo

A yachting marina on Nanaimo harbour's waterfront

Keith, Alison and Heather on a walk around Nanaimo harbour

A final photo of the view from our room's window
at the Coast Bastion Hotel

8

Return Journey

Departed Nanaimo Harbour on Harbour Air Flight 608 at 1:45 p.m. on September 6th

Arrived South Vancouver Seaplane Terminal at 2:05 p.m. – just a short hop as planned!

Departed Vancouver Airport at 5:50 p.m. on Air Canada Flight AC 854

Arrived London Heathrow, Terminal 2, at 11:05 a.m. the next day – September 7th

Our return journey was much more straightforward than the outward journey and went generally smoothly and according to plan! Terry and Ann kindly took us and our luggage to the Harbour Air Seaplane Terminal in Nanaimo harbour, where we checked ourselves and the luggage in. We had returned our rental car – a Volkswagen Beetle no less - to the rental company the day before.

The short Harbour Air Seaplane flight and the Air Canada Long Haul flight were fine, with us in our booked "opposite aisle" seats for the long overnight Air Canada flight. Our arrival experience at Heathrow's Terminal 2 (using the Maple Manor Meet and Greet facility – booked with Holiday Extras) should have been better, but then we had a smooth drive back to Cirencester and arrived home at about 2:20 p.m. in the afternoon of Friday September 7th, and in need of a night or two's good sleep!

I managed to take quite a few photos of the return Harbour Air seaplane flight. This is such an unusual means of transport in most other parts of the world, but it is a very useful one between Nanaimo and Vancouver – when the local flying conditions allow!

Photo of the Harbour Air seaplane terminal in Nanaimo harbor

*Taken from my window seat in the Harbour Air seaplane
before take off*

Another photo looking out of the seaplane window before take off

Flying over some kind of coastal freight terminal?

Good advert for Harbour Air - except for the reflection!

Groups of floating logs in transit over the water

Photo of other islands between Nanaimo and Vancouver

We "splashed down" at the Vancouver Seaplane Terminal!

Unloading the luggage at the Vancouver Seaplane Terminal

Two more seaplanes waiting on the water at the Vancouver Seaplane Terminal

Printed in Great Britain
by Amazon

22039857R00078